*This book is dedicated to Martine — my wife,
and to my children, Aude and Clement.*

S A H A R A
MAGIC DESERT

We, natives of the Sahara, nomads or oasis dwellers, recognize through these images the land of our ancestors — perennial, hard, implacable but kind to those who know it, love it, and respect it.

To all those passionately fond of great spaces, the Sahara will always remain the most beautiful desert of the world.

Mano Dayak
Agadez
A notable Tuareg

916.6

Thirty deluxe version printed and numbered
1 to 30 contain an original print signed by the
photographer and equally numbered 1 to 30.

First Edition
ISBN 0-916567-08-7
Copyright ©1986 by J. M. Durou and AGEP.

Published by Arpel Graphics
32 E. Micheltorena
Santa Barbara, California 93101

SAHARA
MAGIC DESERT

JEAN-MARC DUROU

Text by
THEODORE MONOD

Translation by
ANNE and PATRICK O'DOWD

ARPEL

Landscape

Does a marvelous book of images really need a text to evoke all its powers to fascinate and make us dream?

Personally, I am not quite sure, but the photographer and the publisher, anxious to fortify and expand the book's visual message, have expressed the desire to add a few pages of commentary by an old Saharan explorer, who has spent more than 60 years in the desert, both on foot and on camel. This traveler also has worked long in the field of natural science (geology, archaeology, and botany) as well as in geography and history.

Forget for a moment the familiar sights, sounds, and routines of our landscape and day; the familiar garden, the newspaper delivered to our doorstep at dawn, the red bus (or the green) circulating quietly on the street, and the man off to work at 8:30 a.m. Instead, look beyond the limits of the temperate landscapes with its field, its woods, its farms, its cows, and its telephone poles. All this is only one aspect of the world; there is more. There is the strange and quintuple miracle of the ocean, the polar ice, the deserts, the high country, and the great Forest, the real one, which is not a plantation of trees, but the only one deserving an upper-case "F".

Each of these great themes well deserves to be discovered, penetrated, understood, and loved. For what concerns us here – the Saharan Desert, this beautiful book will help convince you.

To help make the discovery of this astonishing universe easier, a few pages of introduction might help.

Let's start at the beginning. We know that the desert means aridity and thus, a certain type of climate. The yearly average rainfall is less than 100-150mm. The desert begins by rarifying life, and at the limit, succeeds in supressing it. This dryness reduces the vegetal cover and tears through it letting the bare ground show between the plants, sometimes even abolishing life across vast surfaces.

The field, the plantation, the park and the garden, are not so bad, of course. But let's acknowledge that the five true wonders of the world are the ocean, the polar world, the hot desert, the mountains and the forest. That is to say, landscapes that owe nothing to human activity, which existed before us and will still be there after us — except alas maybe the Forest when "the Lord of Creation" will have joined it together with dinosaurs and ammonites in the cemetaries of evolution.

Ocean and desert have much in common. Some gigantic deserts are as flat as the sea, landscapes so "planer" that the horizon remains forever circular, allowing us to walk straight ahead for weeks with nothing forcing us to the least deviation.

Few situations are more similar than a lifeboat lost in the ocean and a little caravan quickening its pace toward a remote well, the only small habitable space for 500 kilometers around, in the heart of an immense hostility dangerous, and dried up. One can fall from a lifeboat as well as a caravan, the danger is the opposite, but yet identical — too much water on one hand, too little on the other.

To get well acquainted and to understand, one must see – directly for the privileged, indirectly for those who will discover the desert through the beauty of images. When these are of high quality, when the photographer is also an artist, sensitive to the magic of form and color, the spectator couldn't have a better guide to take up the discovery of what will be for many, a new world, that of the Sahara Desert.

There are many deserts on the surface of the globe, but the Sahara is at the same time the most vast and the most beautiful. However, it is also a gigantic mosaic of distinct regions, each sharing a common aridity, but each richly diversified. Understanding this, one will say the Saharas, rather than the Sahara.

The talented photographer hasn't claimed to gather in this volume all "the elements of a Saharan encyclopedia," but only to offer a simple anthology. The book does not contain images of occidental Sahara, or the stupefying Libyan Desert where one can travel several hundred kilometers without seeing even one dried-up plant, or even the stupendous Tibesti, which culminates high in the sky at 3,415 meters. Instead, these pages are dedicated to Central Sahara, which evoke the principal physical aspects of the Sahara — the adaptation of life to its desertic climate.

On the edges of the desert, vegetation will remain "diffused," while in the heart of the Sahara (except in high country), it will be "concentrated," or progressively limited to the dry stream beds and ravines. Without humus, the soil as commonly understood, the veil of vegetation, which normally masks the stony skeleton of the earth, dwindles or even disappears.

Thereon, the planet is literally laid bare, bereft of skin and flesh, its bones exposed, clean, well-scoured, polished glossy by the wind-born sand.

Let's note in passing that one rarely ever gets dirty in the desert, even without washing. It's when you reach regions with regular rainfall that the ground transforms from pure sand to earth which blackens and stains.

Rocks thus will be bared, exposed to all the agressions of various elements altering it little by little — water (the rain from time to time); sandstorms, the wonderful abrasive which knows so well how to engrave, scour, polish, and even dig the rocks; and variations of temperature, the great heat or intense cold.

Though the result may confound the imagination at the incredible thought of it, the Saharan hydrographic system with its valleys, gorges, and canyons has been slowly, patiently, dug by water — the heritage of a rainy past. The oueds (stream beds) today are at death's door if not dead. Many no longer run and actually are asphyxiated by sand. However, the facts contradict appearances. Fluvial erosion succeeded not only in breaking and cutting the mountains and plateaus, but simultaneously pulverizing and grinding the hardest rocks, ejecting into the distances the debris, blocks, pebbles and sands. These gave way to water and the action of the wind edifying great dunes on the plains.

Let's not forget that erosion is more than running water. Strong rock, sandstone, limestone, and granite withstand the perpetual superficial effects of multiple agents (wind corrosion, dissolution, mechanical actions of the wind or frost). On a human scale, the change cannot be noticed. Twenty thousand years ago only a tiny detail might have been different from the present profile of the high sandstone mound of Adery (Mauritania) which overlooks the sands of Magteir. But with time and duration everything becomes possible, and one day, rather one century, the proud mountain fortress will have disappeared, shoved to the ground. Billions and billions of grams of quartz and sandstone will be liberated to become again the land as they had been before imprisonment in the sandstone.

After all, wasn't this really ancient sand "temporarily" stuck together, and the sand an ancient and future sandstone? "Everything is in everything," the philosopher would say, "and vice-versa," the humorist would add.

As has been said, lack of rain, running water, true soil, and a protective vegetal cover make the desert landscape seem fossilized. Nothing moves, at least to the ephemeral human observer.

The desert, like all the eco-climatic régions, has its own forms and characteristics, largely inherited from a more humid past and maintained by the present aridity in a climate where only the wind still plays an effective role in sculpting the terrestial surface. Thus, it's necessary to define grand morphological types which will be found under a hundred different varieties in the Sahara. By simplifying a great deal, one could designate five major types, five families of actual forms — the mountain mass, the plateau, the "reg" (plain of gravel), the basin, and the dune, though these classifications will be much less distinct.

The mountain masses range in size, from the simple isolated hill ("quelb" or "inselberg") to an entire region of ranges (Iforas, Hoggar, Air, Tibesti). The composition is from the old crystalline base (granite, igneous, etc.) to which volcanic elements, such as basalts, may be superimposed.

The plateau is made of sedimentary rocks (sandstone, limestone, etc.), aligned more or less horizontally. Each is generally limited by cliffs and broken by gorges and canyons. The canyons are often deep and narrow at the bottom and may contain little hidden lakes. The plateau's surface is both a "hammade," paved with rocks, slabs, and sometimes tiny pebbles and "regs" or gravel plains, but perched "regs." Often, in front of the border cliffs, mounds known as "gour" ("zengenberge") are isolated by erosion.

The sand, whether moved by water or wind, is everywhere and in every shape imaginable from a simple veil laid on the ground to a giant edifice able to culminate to a height greater than 100 meters. The shifting dunes are the most difficult of desert forms to study. Describing the multiple types is relatively easy, but determining the genesis of these structures is more difficult, often surrounded by mystery and debate. Whence cometh the sandy material? What are the forces that place it in position and confer its different forms? The answers remain unknown.

The dune has another aspect, its beauty. Who cannot react to the astonishing melange of sharp ridges and sculpted forms, to the brutality and tenderness, to the curves and feminine quality of mounded sands, to the strength and vigor of size and quantity. What of the sand's colors and what of the perfect purity of such noble material, the darkest of which cannot stain?

Surely for the walker and the camel rider, the dune will have its rigors, and on occasion its cruelties; but this will be another story.

Sunrise on the reg of Tademaït.

Sunset on the Djebel Tazat (Tassili n'Ajjer).

Footprints on the dune.

Erg Medjebebat (North of Hoggar).

Erg Medjehebat (North of Hoggar).

*Region of the oued Tin Tarabine (Tassili of Hoggar). A lunar landscape,
the region was abandoned more than 50 years ago after its wells dried up.*

Sand of Tenere.

Strange erosions: rocks of Tassili of Hoggar.

The Koudia Range. Center of the Atakor (Hoggar).

Dunes of the Arakao (East of Air).

Dunes of Temet (Northeast of Air).

Mount Greboun. In the foreground, the dunes of Temet (Northeast of Air).

Dunes of the erg Admer in the Region of Zaoutalaz (Fort Gardel).

Pillars of basalt rising above the oued Tanget (Hoggar).

Region of Essendilene on the edge of the erg Admer (Tassili n'Ajjer).

Near the Adrar Bous, north of the Air,
a rocky space, lost island in the middle of sand dunes.

The Koudia Range in the center of Hoggar.

Dunes of the erg Medjehebat (North of the Hoggar).

Dunes of the erg Medjehebat (North of the Hoggar).

A few kilometers away from the oasis starts the erg Admer,
a magnificent dune range longer than 300 kilometers.

Range of the Tefedest (North of the Hoggar).

Sunrise at the site of Assekrem.

*Assekrem Region of the Atakor
in the center of the mountains of the Hoggar.
Winter nights can be freezing, and the thermometer
sometimes is below -5°C. It is also the domain of the
moufflon who is occasionally visible.*

Mountain of the Hoggar close to Tamanrasset.

Life

The desert isn't as one might think, a land devoid of life without plants and without animals, but rather a land where life is simply rarified by aridity.

As we know, life cannot exist without water, and a mammal subjected to dehydration, bereft of liquid, will eventually die of thirst. Certain species are favored — the dromadery can stand a loss of water equal to 20-30% of its weight; man only 10%.

But if regarded closely, not through the eyes of a simple tourist, but through those of a naturalist, there are more species of plants and animals in the Sahara than you could have imagined. Using vertebrates as an example, we can find 20 species of fish; 10 of amphibians, 90 reptiles (tortoise – 5, lizards – 54, serpents – 31), 116 different mammals, and about 60 nesting birds, and hundreds of migrating birds.

Naturally, the species that succeed in prospering, or at least surviving in the desert, are those who have adapted through their morphology, physiology and biology to the various Saharan environments. Therefore, the aquatic fauna are necessarily very poor, but does exist in temporary ponds (sometimes hosting a profusion of shellfish varieties, the eggs of which can withstand desiccation), or permanent natural cisterns, known as "queltas" or "aquelmans" which can harbor diverse fish (sheatfish, barbels, etc.), shrimp, and occasionally jellyfish (Tibesti, Mauritania). Crocodiles don't appear to have survived the Sahara and today subsist only in Sahel (Mauritania, Ennedi).

In reality, the current fauna are only the weak remains of much more important animal life present only a few thousand years ago, in a less arid Sahara, a kind of weedy, woody savanna where shepherds, fishermen, and farmers could live.

Traces abound of the ancient fauna. First, there are bones and sometimes even whole animal skeletons found in the dried, hardened muds of long-gone lakes: giraffes, elephants, hippopotamus, antelopes, crocodiles, turtles, fish, countless shells, etc; some vertebretes of "perch" show, by their size, animals of about 1.5 meters that would have been unable to live in simple ponds without depth.

Another rich gallery of extinct or rarified species is provided through the sometimes plentiful painted or engraved figurations by neolithic and protohistoric man. These depict elephant, rhinoceros, giraffe, oryx, mufflons, ostrich, and others.

Few things are more moving than discovering, in the midst of a terrible no-man's land, a lake *bottom dry for thousands of years, yet full of remains of aquatic fauna of long ago. On its rim, are neolithic trash heaps of prehistory, debris of consumed animals, bone harpoons, and hooks fashioned from the dorsal plates of crocodiles.*

With closed eyes, one might imagine little gardens of grain crops on the humid, sandy river banks, and on the lake, a flotilla of slim dug-out canoes, with oars moving to the rhythm of fishermen singing. Our eyes open again, and there is an instant awareness of a landscape burnt by the sun, sad sands, and a few rare tufts of grasses so hard that a camel chewing them emits a metallic sound. And one would face five to six hundred kilometers of nothingness before the next well . . . Yes, the Bible has not lied: "and the world passeth away." John I 2, v. 17.

Rough country, this Sahara, where only those organisms that discover ways of resisting the threats of the desertic climate — the temperature extremes (sand as hot as 80°C. surface temperature and freezes of below -18°C. at Tibesti), the violent wind — will succeed in surviving.

Many animals avoid the direct heat through nocturnal activity, spending the day in burrows, both cooler and more humid than the exposed surface. For example, this is the case with rodents.

Many species find water either in their prey (carnivores) or in plants (herbivores). Grain-eating birds have to reach water where some, like the pintailed grouse, bring humidity to their young by wetting their belly feathers.

The beautiful addax antelopes, best adapted of the hoofed animals, live and prosper in the sandy immensity of the "Majabat al-Koubra." Here, because the ground is permeable, there will never be, even following rain, free water. The addax thus drinks while eating, grazing on the few plants growing in its habitat. Afterwards, its stomach contains water and plant material, some of which mixes into a type of vegetal gruel. The ingested water though not very clear remains drinkable as a green and sweetish juice. The addax hunters oblige their camels to ingurgitate the vegetal gruel of the first stomach. Nothing must be lost in the desert.

Plants in the Sahara do not enjoy an easy existence. Whereas animals move either vertically or horizontally over the ground, and plants, once germinated, are irrevocably fixed in position. The aridity places their lives in jeopardy. Thus plants must defend themselves by cunningly limiting losses in water through evaporation. For example, a Saharan plant may have fewer and smaller leaves, or thickened cuticles, or may cover itself with hair, hide its openings, or lengthen its roots to reach underground moisture.

This first group defines itself, if one can say that, by taking up the challenge of dryness and giving battle. But another category of plants choose a different strategy. Rather than adapting structure, these flora limit life cycles to the short favorable period following rains, when moisture is present for weeks or even months. In fact, some species are capable of germinating, growing, blooming, and producing fruit in a few days.

Though the plant has ripened its fruit, the struggle continues because seeds for the next generation must be distributed. How can the seeds be preserved while waiting for the next shower six months or a year or more in the future? What a worry for the parents! The solution is often quite varied and ingenious.

The simplest, but not necessarily the most efficient solution, is to trust the wind. Without any doubt, there are associated risks such as the blowing seeds of sand-based plants onto a field of pebbles or, conversely, rock-growing seeds blowing into the dunes. Sending forth huge quantities of seeds usually ensures that some will be left in the right place when the rain finally falls.

Some fruits' seeds germinate only when wet. Until that time they are kept in reserve on the mother plant. Other seeds moistened by rain, secrete a sticky gum, a kind of glue which makes them stick to the ground. Some graminaceous plants literally screw their fruit into the gum which is then covered with a silvery quivering gauze made out of a myriad of feathery juxtaposed bones. Other seeds will be swallowed by an animal and then traveling through the digestive tract will be deposited through the animal's excrement.

Other fruits or their seeds are fashioned with barbed silk, thorns, or hooks, affixing themselves to the sandal of a wandering nomad or to a camel's foot. In the Magteir dunes (Mauritania), I was able to count 70 fruits attached by their thorns to a nomad's sandals.

Since the Sahara also has known humid times, the last between 6,000-12,000 years ago, it's not surprising that humans inhabited the area perhaps for hundreds of thousands of years. Traces of this co-existence during the stone age are sometimes in prodigious abundance. On the corridor-like gravel fields separating the dune strips south of the Egyptian sandsea, one can find thousands of beautiful bifacial tools *of an evolved Paleolithic culture. They are carved in wood or bone and of a remarkable treatment. A close look reveals that one side is shiny, polished by the blowing sand, while the side resting on the ground is dull and unpolished. The formidable and invitable conclusion is that this abandoned object from more than 100,000 years ago has never been displaced, finding itself in exactly the same position as when remote ancestors discarded it — a pebble unturned out for thousands of years. What a discovery for an animal as ephemeral as the Homo Sapien!*

And today, this sandsea of some 80,000 square kilometers, this dune mound as big as Belgium and Holland, devoid of watering holes and vegetation, maintains only one living inhabitant, a small apterous mantis seen running on the sand, its color hiding it so efficiently that it can be spotted only when moving. How could we imagine here a "normal" country, moist with trees, giraffes, antelopes, elephants, and perhaps men?

How would these men have appeared? What was the color of their skin? Which language did they use? Were they making jokes? We may never know.

But what we can ascertain is that, more recently, 3,000 to 6,000 years ago, prehistoric Saharans took care to carve painted images on cliffs and rocks, representing what they had seen, and in doing so supplied future generations with a catalog of the exhibition. Earliest drawings depict tropical animals, elephants, giraffes, rhinoceros, hippopotamus, and crocodiles. Later in proto-historical time, pictures demonstrated knowledge and uses of metal and horses with beam and yoke. Even later we note the awareness of camels, a sign that the present aridity was beginning.

Some regions of the Sahara are particularly rich in rupicolous figurations. These include the famous Tassali of Ajjers of course, and also the Fezzan, the South-Ornais, Mauritania, the Air, the Tibesti, the Djebel Uweinet, etc.

With the "camel" period often called "libyan-berbere," appear inscriptions in "tifinar" characters and in the central and occidental Sahara. Present day Tuaregs still use these characters.

*In the middle of the dunes of the Tenere, life seems to cling desperately
to where nothing can live; acacia in the middle of dunes.*

*Oued Serssouf (Tassili n'Ajjer). A few Kilometers away from Zaouatalaz
(Fort Gardel), the nomads believe that the stream bed is
inhabited by evil genii; the Tuareg never camp there.*

Essendilene (Tassili n'Ajjer).
In the shade of these canyons where water is
practically always present, nature has regained its rights;
tiny green spaces in the desert immensity.

Canyons of the Tamrit plateau (Tassili n'Ajjer).

*Gueltas of the oued Serssouf. There are many of them
in the Sahara, some shelter a residual aquatic fauna
consisting of sheat-fish and barbels.*

Pink Laurel on the Tamrit Plateau (Tassili n'Ajjer).
It is a deadly plant for the camel who might inadvertantly eat it.

Cypress of the Tamrit plateau (Tassili n'Ajjer).
These trees live today only in the Tassili Range
and are proof of a once green Sahara; some are more than 2,000 years old.
Protected and catalogued to about 300, they survive but don't reproduce
anymore because of the dryness.

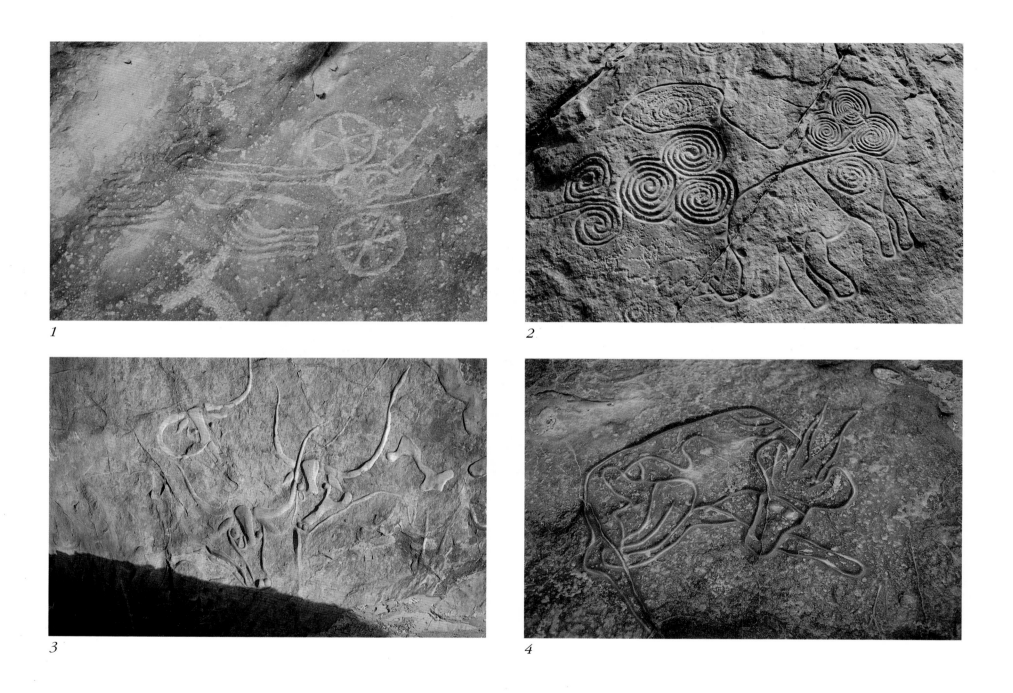

1. *Engravings on the oued Djerat (Tassili n'Ajjer). War wagons. The galloping horses are wonderfully well-represented. In the back, the driver is standing and at the same time holding the reins and his spear.*

2. *Spiral of the oued Djerat. Located in the north of Tassili n'Ajjer, this oued is one of the high places of Saharan pre-history. Engravings are plentiful for miles around. These spirals are the symbols of water and fecundity. They are often found next to wild animals such as giraffes and rhinoceros, evidence of a once green Sahara.*

3. *Oxen of Terrarart (Tassili n'Ajjer). A few Kilometers away from the oasis of Djanet, on the wall of a big isolated boulder, prehistoric men left us as a witness of their presence, one of the most beautiful engravings in the Sahara. Cut in a deep and polished line, these oxen are also called "oxen at the watering place" for their heads are turned toward the ground, and whenever water is running out, their muzzles are flush with the water.*

4. *Marvelous little antelope engraved in the oued Dider (Tassili n'Ajjer). The artist of prehistoric times shows us here the animal at rest, retiring within himself.*

Engraving of the oued Tezirzek (Northeast of the Air Range).
In archeology, defined under the name of "libyan-warriors," these individuals are
noted for their round heads surmounted by feathers and carrying javelin and shield.

1

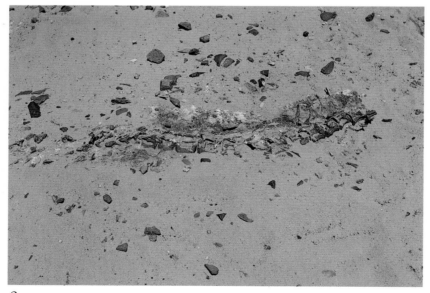

2

1. *Polished hatchet of the Tenere left on the ground.*
   Weapons and tools of neolithic man.

2. *Fossilized fish which yesterday had to be a lake.*
   (Adrar Bous, Northeast of the Air).

Very close to Djanet, a pre-islamic tomb (Libyan-berbere funerary monument).

1. In the center of the Tassili n'Ajjer, the Tamrit plateau offers a great open air museum. The site of Tin-Zamaitak gives us descriptive rupestriac paintings, as well as magical (mufflons, jellyfish, and individuals decorated with paint).

2. Rupestral paintings of Tassili n'Ajjer. The period from 6000 to 1200 B.C. The colors are from ocre contained in iron oxide, goat milk, and sap from acadias.

3. Paintings of Tin-Tazarift (Tassili n'Ajjer). Prehistoric pirogue. Its shape, especially its prow, is reminiscent of the canoes of ancient Egypt.

4. Paintings representing dromedaries (Tassili n'Ajjer). The appearance of the camel corresponds to the final period of drying up. From now on only this animal can make life possible in these great desertic places.

*North of the Hoggar, the mountain range of Tefedest is also an important
rupestral center. It is difficult to get to this place, and to visit it one must start
from the cultural center of Mertoutek. The paintings represent scenes from life
that make us think of the camps of the Nigerian peulhs-bororos tribes.*

Guelta d'Iherir (Tassili n'Ajjer).
This guelta was the last one to shelter a crocodile,
a surviver from the Sahara when it was green.

Oued Tezirzek (Northeast of the Air Range).
There are years when it is not rare to see several gazelle herds a day.

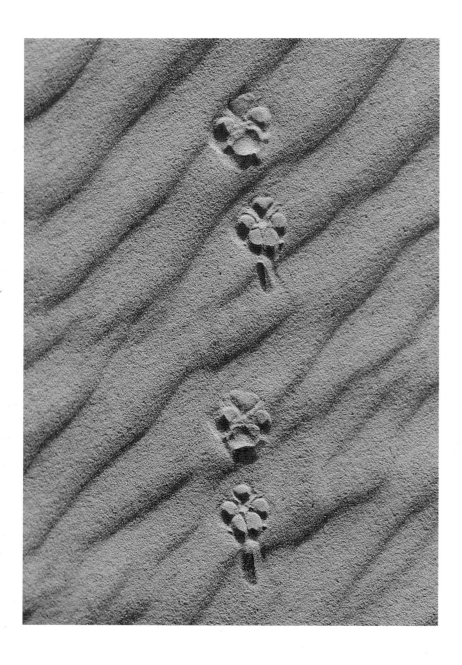

Jackal footsteps.
Gazelle herd. Dunes of Temet (Air).

Ostriches in the oued Zagado (Mount Air).
In the last century, ostriches were scattered all over the Sahara.
Having been hunted for so many years, they now live only in south Sahara.

*Here, the desert ends. Abalak Lake located in the
Nigerian Sahel is the furthest southern limit where
Tuareg nomads come to water their cattle.*

Oued Tanget (Hogger).
Now dried up, this stream bed, if ever the rain
starts falling, in a few minutes becomes transformed
into a bubbling stream.

The Oasis

As previously suggested, the ocean and desert share many similarities. In terms of human settlement, symmetry stares us in the face. In effect, the sea allows only a sedentary life, rooted on its islands — the ocean oasis. In the same way, the palm grove is the true Saharan island. Beyond these life-sustaining spaces, existence requires an obligatory mobility, the wanderer and the set-course, the double road of the nomad and the seafarer.

Oasis implies water, but means much more to the desert wanderer. Thousands of wells pierce the surface of the desert, yet the oasis is peculiar and special. It is a place of revitalization because the nomad doesn't live from the desert. Many elements of his material existence, whether linked to his diet or not, come from without, sometimes from afar (tea, sugar, cloth, etc.). Thus, from time to time the nomad will necessarily "touch earth" to resupply himself with cereals, sugar, and teas (now indispensable), material, or metallic objects. The oasis then is both a palm grove and a store, a market in the shadow of a date palm tree.

Things are not always so simple. There is the intermediate case of the traveling merchant selling goods in the encampments.

Then there is the fundamental opposition between the house and the tent. For within the palm grove, no matter how miserable and bug-invested, is a village with buildings made of dried earth or stone, portraying permanence and immobility as its most fundamental characteristic. A tent is movable — that is its purpose! A hut will never move.

Naturally, a village might be abandoned and structures fall into ruin. The little city of Teghaza, constructed out of salt blocks and deserted in the 17th Century is one example. Emerging from sand on the edge of a rock-salt mine, traces of its houses, foundation walls, and even an archtectural arc are still standing in a site so desolate that never again will an archeologist be able to pursue serious diggings.

Besides, it would be a mistake to think that sedentary life necessarily implies the palm grove. A village can be created in a site which is economically favorable; near a rock-salt mine (Taoudeni), around wells situated on a busy path (Araouan, Amrennan in the Tanezouft), on a defensive uprising in the land (neolithic villages along the cliffs of Tichitt), and sometimes around an important religious figure, who deep in the desert, has created a religious center.

However, the "normal" oasis is the palm grove with its forest of date palms surrounded at their base by gardens of barley, wheat, and vegetables with often a few fruit trees (apricot, pomogranate, or orange, etc.) The charm and poetry of these peaceful gardens enfold the visitor in softened palm shadows, leaves rustling above in the wind as one walks through narrow winding alleys, edged by walls of earth or hedges.

The palm grove always has water, a running source distributed by an infinity of little canals according to ancient and definite rules. Water comes from wells, sometimes artisan, or springs, or underground galleries the length of which confounds the imagination. Opening and maintaining wells represents a colossal effort if we take into account the means used —pickaxe, hoe, basket, and in the past, slavery.

For the camel-driver who at last sees the black line of the palm grove on the horizon, the oasis represents commercial opportunities to buy and sell, multiple social contacts, news to exchange, the temporary security of abundant available water; and then the courtship possibilities must be considered. Besides, isn't the harbor the same thing for the sailor?

Port-oasis or port village? During the great camel-drives, men and animals trek for weeks between wells. The tent remains portable and will be loaded and unloaded on a camel.

The ship moving across the sea anchors infrequently, much as the nomad of the Sahara traveling the ocean of pebbles and sand. However, both usually have a fixed destination, harbor for one, oasis for the other, and both will be underway again after respite.

On arrival, the real nomad ventures with apprehension through small winding paths as a blind man between opaque walls where the camel too is often afraid. The Saharan traveler must find a place to camp, feed his animals, (and horrible scandal) buy wood at the market, avoid village robbers and greedy shopkeepers. Thus, with business done he will, with a sense of relief, come out of the maze of little narrow streets to find once more free space, far away sights, and safety from the world's thieves; and, of course, free wood.

But let's go back to these inhabited centers. In the Occidental Sahara, the old cities of dry stone witness the ravages of time: Chingetti, invaded by sand: Ouadane, in ruin though once a famous Saharan harbor on the road to Morocco; Tichitt, where brownstone and blue-green schists made for remarkable facade ornamentation; and more eastward at Oualata where a more peculiar style of decoration with dark-red elements developed, and an urban life more typical for us with evolved types of furniture (lamps, clay pots for perfumes, etc.).

In the south of Algeria, the cities of Hzab testify to a true urban civilization, expressing a complex social structure, attributable to a religious group which has guarded its strong personality for centuries.

Aerial view of Erg Issaouane north of Tassili n'Ajjer.
Each of these dunes has an average height of 200 meters.
The range extends over 300 kilometers in length.

Palm grove at the foot of the grand erg occidental (Saoura). Ghardaia.

Morning light on this village of the Beni Abbes Region (Saoura).

Several cities form the M'Zab (Beni-Isguen, Bounoura, El Ateuf, Melika, Berriane, Guerrara). Ghardaia is the capital.

Oasis of Ghardaia: Capital of M'Zab.

Archway around the marketplace of Ghardaia
protecting the small shops from the sun.

Streets of Ghardaia (M'Zab).

*In the street of Ghardaia, sheltered from the sun,
there is a perpetual commercial activity. Older men left alone
devote their time to praying and palavering.*

Rampart of Bounoura, one of the seven cities of M'Zab.
The palm trees sprouted at the foot of the rampart.

Lane in Ghardaia leading to the mosque.
Five times a day, the minaret rising above
the city, launches the call to prayer.

Ghardaia Market — Oasis of M'Zab.
The Mozabites are tradesmen with the
best reputation in the central Sahara.

Young girls of the oasis of Ideles (Hoggar).
Ramadan fasting (a Moslem celebration) ends up with high festivities.

Agadez (Nigeria). This city is the meeting ground of Saharan and Black African populations. Famous because of its architecture, especially its XVI Century minaret, Agadez is also the only town to have maintained its sultan.

Minaret of the oasis of Metili.
Very close to M'Zab, this oasis is the capital of an important tribe,
the "Chaambas." This tribe from the north Sahara (nomad and
half nomad) has a past of war and religion that makes it
one of the most prestigious tribes.

Haoussa house of a rich Agadez tradesman.

Oasis of Djanet (Tassili n'Ajjer). On the occasion of the Zeziba festival,
women gather and sing, giving rhythm to the men's dance.

The oasis of Iherir (Tassili d'Ajjer) is inhabited by sedentary tuareg.
Lost in the middle of cliffs, it is charming.

Oasis of El Golea. The palm tree is the most important of the oasis;
its dates provide food, its trunk is used as building material,
and its shade provides a place for a garden.

Child of the Kanouri tribe in the oasis of Bilma (Kaouar).

*Goulimine Market. Currently animals are brought from camp to camp.
A big market such as this is unusual. Only the great markets
of occidental Sahara have important camel gatherings.*

Wheat field in the oasis of Timia (Air Range).

Guelta of the oasis of Timia.
A permanent water hole in the heart of the Air Mountains.

Camel saddles being made for the nomads.
Agadez is the most active Saharan crafts center.

*Young boys from the oasis of Bounoura; their heads are covered with
a white "chechia," a distinctive sign of mozabite people.*

Cheikh Sidi Aissa's tomb dominates the little town of Melika,
nicknamed the "queen of the cities" of the M'Zab.

Summer villa in a palm grove of the M'Zab.

Palm groves of Timia (Air Range).

Tamanrasset's streets (Hoggar).

For a long time unknown, the Tassili of Hoggar are today being visited by numerous touristic expeditions.

The Nomad

Nomads, the eternal desert wanderers, profess many variations in lifestyle. Some are seasonal, associated with herding goats, sheep or cattle in search of greener pastures. Others are the great camel-driving nomads of the Sahara such as the Requibats of the Western Sahara. The commonality, however, is the use of easily dismantled and carried dwellings — sometimes a tent, sometimes mat huts common in Tibesti and Sahel.

Nomamdic life, as its first principle, is an adaptation to conditions imposed by the desert milieu, particularly, the rarity of waterholes, the fluctuations of the vegetal cover, and the variations in rainfall.

The two major elements conditioning the nomad's life are water and available grazing ground which, unfortunately, are not always associated. Good pasture can't be used if there is no water, and full wells are useless where there is no usable vegetation for the herds. However, in winter, the association of water and grazing is less critical, as camel herds can exploit excellent pastures for months without need of a watering place. In these instances, the shepherd slaves who guard the animals live primarily on the milk of their animals. As the hot season approaches, the shepherd must bring the herd closer to the wells.

Rainfall in the Sahara no longer maintains a seasonal regularity or balance. The yearly variability lacks significant averages between two "good" showers (the kind which will wet the sand a couple of feet down). In the Libyan Sahara, for example, it might rain significantly only every 10 to 15 years or longer.

Without water, the hardy perennial species, such as woody plants will die. And the herbaceous plants born with the rain, will provide pasturage for at most a few months. These admirable green grazing grounds known as "acheb" or "rbia" are appreciated greatly by nomads and their animals.

Shepherds must search endlessly for better pasture and must move herds and camps great distances. Only through this process can the nomad of the Sahara survive in the heart of this bio-climatic milieu as hostile as the artic regions in many ways. Thus, one must appreciate the ecological success story of the great camel drivers as a feat of strength just as extraordinary as feats of the Eskimos of Baffin Island.

The nomadic shepherds face social as well as environmental challenges. The central governments have no special sympathy for these free men. Often, these agencies think it necessary to direct a policy of imposed *seditarisation, without acknowledging the link uniting nomadism and the desertic eco-climate. However, it is not effectual to recommend to a Saharan nomad to abandon his millenarian specialization and devote himself to the cultivation of carrots or potatoes. For him the dilemma is not between the pasture and the kitchen-garden, but between the pasture and . . . nothing. His lifestyle and techniques are not the result of choice between possibilities, but the necessary adoption of the only possible method for the exploitation of natural resources.*

How do they live, these nomads with dwellings which must be mobile and packable?

There are, even within the Sahara, several types of tents. First the "classic" type, which is brown and oblong and made from bands of crude linen woven with hair. When flat on the ground, it is creased upward where its center is supported by two strong masts. A lighter variant which is white in color is made from cotton.

The leather tent is a compound of up to one hundred goat skins sewn together. Its roof rests on stakes, and empty spots are filled with mats. This shelter of skins is typical of the Tuareg, but is found in other Saharan populations, such as the Berabiches.

The fixed straw hut or "tikit" of sedentary peoples has a framework of wooden arches and a blanket of rugs. Its shape is more or less circular.

My father used to say with reason, "We're all possessed by our possessions...." It's a danger that a nomad could never know because material goods must be reduced to the simplest expression of necessity. In addition, the quantity must be limited to the back of one camel, or perhaps two in rare cases.

Let's walk into a tent to discover the furniture. The inventory will be quickly completed, as there are very few items: a mat on the ground, a few polychrome rugs for the richer, a small wooden chest for precious objects (jewels for example), a few leather or linen bags, water-skins (all carefully hung), and other smaller skins for buttermilk or butter. In the kitchen, there is a flat millstone and a sloping one with its small pestle, cast-iron and earthen cooking pots, basins and bowls made of wood, enamel or brass, one or two wooden funnels, a kettle and the necessary objects for the tea ceremony (green tea of course), including a pewter or enameled tea pot, small glasses, and a sugar box. Food is kept in bags (dates, millet, wheat, watermelon seeds, and dried tomatoes). A hatchet will complete this poor list with, of

Panorama of Assekrem (Hoggar).

Dunes of erg Admer (Tassili n'Ajjer).

Every year the Tuareg make caravans (the Tarlment) and go across the Tenere to reach the Kaouar, land of the rock salt mine. During two or three months this trip will perpetuate one of the oldest African trades; millet versus salt. During these 700 kilometers of distance covered, they will find only two wells, and the food necessary to the trip is loaded before they start.

*North of the Air, the oasis of Iferouand stands
against the mountain range of Tamgak.
Behind this rocky mass starts the huge Tenere.*

Tuareg of Kel Tadele Tribe at the foot of the big dune of Arakao, east of the Air.

Tuareg blacksmith from Tamanrasset.
Blacksmith's form their own cast through which tradition
relates them to the masters of fire. They are at the same time
despised and feared for their knowledge.

Tuareg woman from Kel Fadey tribe (Tamesna Region).

Wells in the plain of Talak (Mount Air).
Young Tuareg girls. The young girl on the right has a hairdo
symbolizing the scorpion; the representation of the stinger
can be seen at the base of the nape of the neck.

Nomads selling their goats in Abalak market (Nigeria).
The animals are the only true money for exchange to buy
millet and needed cloth for camp life.

Wells of Amalawlaw, in the Gall Region (Nigeria).
Here, a Tuareg is waiting for his turn to water his animals.
The cattle are numerous and the tribes different:
Peulhs, Arabs, and Tuareg keep close around the wells.

Tuareg from the Kel Oui Tribe (Air Range).
The preparation of green tea is a true ceremony for the nomads.

When the herd comes back from pasture, the Tuareg get busy
around the well to water their animals. Here in the Air, water is only a few meters
from the ground, but in other regions, it is not rare to find
wells reaching a depth of more than 60 meters.

Camel rider at Tamanrasset. The end of Ramadan is the occasion for religious festivities during which the Tuareg gather to participate in great camel races.

*Tuareg of the Dag Rali Tribe. They wander in the region of Atakor
in the center of Hoggar. The turban which covers their heads varies
according to the taste of each individual. Some carry turbans
which are more than twelve meters long.*

Tuareg camp in the Hoggar. Adjou n'Telbe tribe.

Tuareg woman from the Adjou n'Telbe tribe in her camp (Hoggar).
According to the region and the wealth of the nomads, Tuareg tents
are made of different sizes of mufflon or goat skin.
Under the vellum of the skin, they put around the "assaber," a mat made out of
very tight marcouba stems touched up with colored leather.

During the hot middle afternoon, men talk and joke under the tent.
The humorous qualities of the Tuareg contrast with the harshness of the climate.

The Tuareg children of the Kel Fadey Tribe (Tamesua Region).
Until the age of puberty, young boys don't wear veils. Their education
during the day consists of taking care of the herds. When evening comes,
they learn the rules of tribal life from the adults.

Djanet Tuaregs preparing themselves for the Sebiba. This dance is based on the rhythm of great drums or gangas that the women beat. Men wear the takoumbout, an enormous red "chechia" put on their indigo turban. In their hand, they hold the takouba, a Tuareg sword which allows them to mime fighting during the dance.

Tuareg camel rider. Illizi Region (Tassili d'Ajjer).
Warriors in the early XX Century;
the nomads are still very attached to their weapons.

At the first rays of dawn,
the Gani's feast gives rise to great camel ricing.

Air Tuareg getting ready for the race.

*On the ceremonious occasions, Tuaregs organize the Ilougan. Women gather
in circles pounding the tindi (drum) and chant melodies. Camel drivers
turn around them as close and as fast as possible, showing their virtuosity.*

Only in Arab tribes do the women wear veils.
Among the Tuareg of berbere origin it's the men.
Tuareg men must never show their face. The turban
raised to the limit of their eyes is a sign of
great respect toward their interlocutor.

Oasis of Iferouane (North Air).
To the rhythm of the tindi, Iferouane Tuareg women sing old time melodies
in chorus. The men won't be long in joining them, enlarging the circle.

A young Tuareg girl of the Kel Fadey Tribe (Tamesna).
The tindi resonates to the accompaniment of clapping hands, suddenly the voice
of a favored soloist arises out of the chorus, the others follow.

Young Tuareg woman of Kel Fadey (Nigeria).

To participate in a ceremony, it is not unusual for a nomad to travel more than 200 kilometers. These festivities are an occasion for the aged to meet again and for the young to find romance.

*A young Tuareg girl adorned with her most beautiful jewelry
on the occasion of the Gani festivities. (Tamesna).*

*Tuareg camel drivers race in the oasis of Iferouane.
(North of Aïr). Such a large gathering of camel drivers
is highly unusual because of dry pastures
which tend to spread out the camps.*

In the great plains north of Tamesna, the herd lengthen out in their search for new pastures (Northwest of Air).

Sandstorm on the dunes of Tenere (Adrar Chiriet Region).

Erg Medjehebat (North of the Hoggar).

Erg Medjehebat dunes.

*Sculpted by erosion, the rocks on the Tassili n'Ajjer plateau form.
Because of their number, they form a maze
where one can find hundreds of rupicolous paintings.*

Sunrise on the Erg Occidental.

Evening light on the reg rising above the oued Tanget, Hoggar Range.

About eighty kilometers from Tamanrasset, in the heart of the Hoggar Range,
the site of Assekrem is one of the most beautiful in the Sahara.
At 2,700 meters high, Father Foucauld had settled his hermitage
which today is still inhabited by its priests.

Landscape in the center of the Air Mountains.
The abundant summer rain makes the landscape even more green.
This explains why the Air was named "Switzerland Sahara"
in the Nineteenth Century by some explorers who crossed it.

A piece of advice for beginning camel drivers

The first louse is a big one, of course : Pediculus Vestimenti. Don't be shocked. One doesn't sleep with the bedouins with impunity. But comfort yourself : it's only the first one...

You will realize, once you arrive at camp that on the way you dropped the can of butter, your best pair of sandals, the only ones that were comfortable. Don't say "that tops all". Patience. Sooner or later you'll top that.

Resign yourself ahead of time to seeing your possessions break up slowly — or quickly — but no doubt about it, relentlessly. Don't protest, get accustomed to the rule that "Things of this world pass"... as the Scriptures say. One can learn this here better than anywhere else.

And also, if you don't want to dent your kettle or lose its lid, or break your straps, tear your pants, or destroy your glasses, just stay home. What are you doing in the country of brutal caravans ?

Take with you a bit of soap and a toothbrush, one never knows. But believe me, I'll bet you'll never touch neither one nor the other. Sahara is the only country where one can remain clean for months without ever washing.

The day you decide to strike camp, the work begins at dawn because what you're doing seems very important to you, very urgent, and because you belong to a world which doesn't serenely lose time. There will be a difficulty — a camel who makes believe it's lost for example. This to teach you the vanity of your agitations. Don't become irritated, it doesn't help. Don't be foolishly in a hurry, the day is long... and there is tomorrow...

Think of everything in advance and in detail, but don't dream empty dreams. One always forgets something and something very important.

And then, don't take measures beforehand. Reality will have fun thwarting your plans. Before all foresee the unforeseeable, the great master for all of us is the desert. Who could have ever imagined that you would be stopped by thirty-six stormy hours of rain and hail ?

No, it is not "pleasant", no more than the spit of camel regurgitation, ticks in your pants, spoiled or brackish water, tasteless gruel, windy nights, toenails in freezing sand and other similar "joyful things". The sources of annoyance in this life are copious, tremendous. But there are consolations, the size of its cruelties. And this is our revenge for them, the initiated will understand me.

Don't let yourself be had : for the baas of sheep, a hoped for shelter (and dark colored, it will be discovered from far away by an experienced eye), the hope of a cup of milk, a meal with meat, a crack at an unattended love affair, your people will explain to you that it is best to stop at 10:00 a.m. to camp, and let the animals eat, for without food... it's the last pasture, nothing left ahead... but beware : sometimes it's true. So hard. No real rules. As usual, an alternating series of mistakes which make up for each other.

Is the noon rest scorching ? Is the shade of this thorn bush thin ? The sand burning ? These broken stones sharp and unstable ? The water evil smelling ? The wind fiendish ? This night freezing ? Don't complain. There is nobody to hear you or feel sorry for you. Endure. Be patient. Clench your teeth. Sooner or later your revenge will come.

What's more, I know you well. When this so long wanted revenge will arrive at last, when you will lay satisfied with delicate food, refreshed with colorless water, without goat hair, in a sybarite bed, all warm under a roof, then, instead of savoring your bliss for long, as soon as the extreme tiredness of your solitary walk will be forgotten, then you will surprise yourself by missing those hard distances, your worn feet, your blistered lips, your sleep curled up under the stars.

And the first occasion which arrives will be the one where you'll start again...

Dunes in the blue mountains of Izouzadene (Northeast of the Air Range).

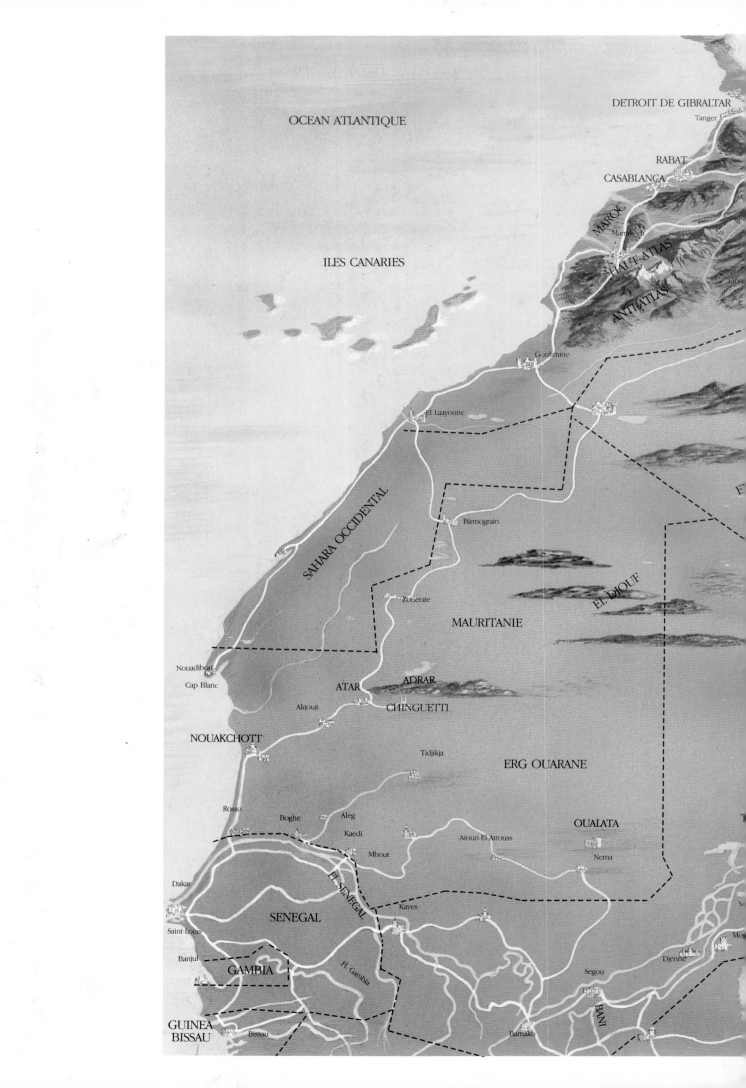

ALGER
Oran
ATLAS TELLIEN
TUNIS
ATLAS SAHARIEN
Biskra
Massif de l'Aures
El-Djem
Sfax
Chott Melrhir
Souf
Tozeur
Gabes
Aïn-Sefra
Touggourt
Nefta
Kebili
GHARDAIA
Temacine
El-Oued
TUNISIE
TRIPOLI
Leptis Magna
Béchar
Taghit
OUARGLA
Hassi-Messaoud
Bengasi
BENI-ABBES
GRAND ERG OCCIDENTAL
EL-GOLEA
Rhadames
Hamada El Hamra
Kerzaz
TIMIMOUN
GRAND ERG ORIENTAL
El Ksar
Gourara
PLATEAU TINHERT
Hassi-Belguebbour
Ohanet
EL-GUERARA
Adrar
ALGERIE
In-Amenas
LIBYE
PLATEAU TADEMAIT
Reggane
Mandara
Sebha
Touat
IN-SALAH
Amguid
Garama
Ubari
MURZUQ
Plaine du TIDIKELT
TASSILI N'AJJER
Arak
Amadror
GHAT
Tefedest
Zaouatallaz
(FORT GARDEL)
Ilhet
Waw an Namus 538
Kufra
Mertoutek
Tamrit
TAHAT 2918
Ideles
DJANET
Asseksem
ERG D'ADMER
TANEZROUFT
Tazrouk
HOGGAR
Foucauld 2885
Aigs. Sissé 3265
Abalessa
ATAKOR
MT GAUTHIER
Toussidé
TIBESTI
Bidon V.
Tit
Wour
AOZOU
TAMANRASSET
Au Natron 2500
ADRAR DES IFORAS
BARDAI
Plateau Djado
ZOUAR
Aguelhok
3415 Emi Koussi
TASSILI DU HOGGAR
KIDAL
TENERE
SEGUEDINE
Borkou
Plateau Erdi
Arlit
TEMET
Mourdisenke
BILMA
IFEROUANE
Mt. AIR
Ennedi 1450
Fada
TIMIA
Fachi
NIGER
Tegguidda
GAO
N'Tessoum
Djourab
In Gail
AGADES
Gr. ERG.BILMA
NIGER
TAHOUA
Tanout
Nguigmi
TCHAD
Darfur
Abeche
Niamey
Maradi
Zinder
Bahr El Ghazal
Dj Marra 3024
FASO
Fleuve Niger
(VOLTA)
Dosso
Katsina
Lac
TCHAD
Kukawa
An
Kano
GANA
TOGO
BENIN
N'DJAMENA
AFRIQUE CENTRALE

achevé d'imprimer 2e trimestre 1986
sur les presses de l'imprimerie AGEP-Marseille France
dépôt légal : 32.86   imprimé en France